A Numerology Series

by

Lloyd Leon

EIGHT

Life Path Eight

Contents

Chapter 1

Understanding Life Path 8

The Significance of Life Path Numbers

The significance of life path numbers extends far beyond mere numerological curiosity; they serve as a guiding compass for individuals seeking to navigate their personal and professional lives. For Life Path 8 individuals, this number symbolizes power, ambition, and a strong desire for material success. Understanding the intricacies of the Life Path 8 number can unlock a wealth of potential, allowing individuals to harness their inherent strengths while addressing the challenges they may face. By recognizing the pivotal role that Life Path 8 plays in shaping one's destiny, individuals can strategically align their goals with their innate capabilities.

Life Path 8 is often associated with financial mastery and the pursuit of abundance. This number encourages individuals to cultivate a mindset geared toward prosperity, emphasizing the importance of setting clear financial goals and taking calculated risks. Life Path 8 individuals are naturally inclined toward leadership and entrepreneurship, making it essential for them to understand the significance of their number in relation to wealth creation. By embracing their financial acumen, Life Path 8 individuals can transform their vision into reality, ensuring they not only achieve personal success but also inspire others along the way.

Leadership strategies for Life Path 8 individuals are crucial for maximizing their potential. Those on this path are often seen as natural leaders, possessing the charisma and drive to motivate others. Understanding the significance of their life path number allows them to refine their leadership style, fostering collaboration and empowering team members. Life Path 8 individuals can excel in positions of authority by cultivating emotional intelligence and embracing a visionary approach. This understanding of their leadership potential can lead to greater career advancement and the ability to leave a lasting impact in their chosen fields.

Health and wellness are also vital components of the Life Path 8 journey. The drive for success can sometimes lead to an imbalance in personal well-being, making it essential for Life Path 8 individuals to prioritize self-care. Recognizing the significance of their life path number encourages a holistic approach to health, integrating physical fitness, mental resilience, and emotional stability. By establishing routines that support their well-being, Life Path 8 individuals can sustain their energy and focus, allowing them to pursue their ambitions without sacrificing their health.

Finally, the spiritual growth and development of Life Path 8 individuals can be significantly enhanced by understanding the significance of their number. This path invites individuals to explore deeper philosophical questions about power, responsibility, and legacy. Engaging with these themes can lead to profound personal transformations, enabling Life Path 8 individuals to find purpose beyond material success. By integrating spiritual practices into their lives, they can cultivate a sense of balance, ensuring that their ambitions serve not only their personal goals but also contribute positively to the world around them.

Traits of Life Path 8 Individuals

Life Path 8 individuals are characterized by their strong drive for success and an unwavering ambition that propels them toward achieving their goals. These individuals often possess an innate sense of authority and leadership, enabling them to command respect and inspire others. Their determination is not merely for personal gain; they are often motivated by a desire to make a significant impact in their communities and the world at large. This leadership quality, combined with their strategic thinking, allows them to navigate complex situations with ease, making them natural problem solvers and decision-makers.

Financial mastery is a prominent trait of Life Path 8 individuals. They have a unique relationship with money, often viewing it as a tool for achievement and a means to secure their vision for the future. This perspective drives them to pursue careers that offer financial stability and growth, whether in business, finance, or entrepreneurship. Their ability to recognize opportunities and take calculated risks often leads to significant financial success. However, it is crucial for them to cultivate a balanced approach to finances, ensuring that their pursuit of wealth does not overshadow other important aspects of life, such as relationships and personal well-being.

Health and wellness are critical considerations for Life Path 8 individuals, who may sometimes prioritize work and success over their physical and emotional health. Their ambitious nature can lead to stress and burnout if not managed properly. Engaging in regular self-care practices, such as exercise, meditation, and balanced nutrition, is essential for maintaining their energy levels and overall health. By recognizing the importance of wellness, Life Path 8 individuals can sustain their productivity and effectiveness in all areas of life, allowing them to achieve their goals without sacrificing their health.

In the realm of relationships, Life Path 8 individuals often exhibit strong loyalty and commitment. However, their intense focus on success can sometimes lead to challenges in personal connections. They may struggle with vulnerability, finding it difficult to express their emotions or rely on others. To foster healthy relationships, it is essential for them to practice open communication and emotional intelligence, allowing them to build deeper connections with loved ones. By balancing their ambitious nature with a genuine appreciation for relationships, Life Path 8 individuals can create a supportive network that enhances their personal and professional lives.

Creativity and innovation are also integral traits of Life Path 8 individuals. Their ability to think outside the box and challenge conventional norms enables them to develop unique solutions and drive change in their fields. Embracing their creative side can lead to breakthroughs that not only benefit their careers but also contribute to their legacy. By integrating creativity into their daily lives, Life Path 8 individuals can harness their innovative potential, ensuring that they leave a lasting impact on the world while achieving their personal aspirations.

Common Challenges Faced by Life Path 8

Individuals on Life Path 8 often encounter unique challenges that can impede their journey toward success and fulfillment. One of the most significant hurdles is the pressure to achieve financial success and maintain authority. Life Path 8 individuals are typically driven by ambition and a desire for material wealth, which can lead to an overwhelming sense of responsibility. When financial goals are not met, feelings of inadequacy can arise, causing stress and anxiety. It is essential for those on this path to develop resilience and a healthy relationship with money, viewing it as a tool for empowerment rather than a measure of self-worth.

Leadership, while a natural inclination for Life Path 8 individuals, can also present challenges. The desire to take charge and influence others can sometimes lead to conflicts with peers or subordinates. This can manifest as difficulties in collaboration and communication, creating a perception of being overly authoritative or domineering. To overcome this, it is crucial for Life Path 8 individuals to cultivate emotional intelligence and practice active listening. By fostering a more inclusive leadership style, they can inspire and motivate others while still maintaining their strong sense of direction.

Health and wellness are often neglected by those on Life Path 8 due to their relentless pursuit of success. The tendency to prioritize work and ambition over personal well-being can lead to burnout and health issues. Life Path 8 individuals must recognize the importance of balancing their professional aspirations with self-care routines. Incorporating regular exercise, mindfulness practices, and proper nutrition can significantly enhance their overall well-being. By prioritizing health, they can sustain their energy levels and improve their capacity to achieve their goals.

In the realm of relationships, Life Path 8 individuals may struggle with vulnerability and emotional expression. Their focus on achievement and control can sometimes create barriers in personal connections, leading to feelings of isolation. It is essential for them to understand the value of open communication and emotional intimacy in relationships. By allowing themselves to be vulnerable and nurturing deeper connections, they can create supportive networks that enhance both their personal and professional lives.

Finally, the journey of spiritual growth for Life Path 8 individuals can be fraught with challenges, particularly in reconciling material ambitions with spiritual fulfillment. The quest for financial mastery may overshadow their spiritual pursuits, leaving them feeling unbalanced. To address this, it is vital for Life Path 8 individuals to engage in practices that align their material goals with their spiritual values. This could involve seeking mentorship in spiritual development, exploring philosophical teachings, or participating in community service. By integrating spiritual principles into their daily lives, they can achieve a more harmonious existence that honors both their ambitions and their inner selves.

Chapter 2

Unlocking the Potential of Life Path 8

Identifying Personal Strengths

Identifying personal strengths is a crucial step for individuals on Life Path 8, as it lays the foundation for achieving financial mastery and leadership success. Life Path 8 individuals are often characterized by ambition, resilience, and a strong desire for achievement. To unlock their full potential, they must first engage in self-reflection to pinpoint the innate qualities that set them apart. This process involves introspection and an honest assessment of their skills, talents, and experiences, which can ultimately guide them toward career advancement and personal fulfillment.

One effective method for identifying personal strengths is through the analysis of past experiences. Life Path 8 individuals can reflect on moments when they felt most fulfilled or successful. By examining the skills they utilized during these times, they can uncover patterns that highlight their unique capabilities. Additionally, seeking feedback from trusted peers, mentors, or coaches can provide valuable insights into strengths that may not be immediately apparent. This external perspective can often reveal attributes that Life Path 8 individuals may take for granted, such as their ability to inspire others or their strategic thinking skills.

Another approach is to engage in self-assessment tools, such as personality tests or strength inventories. These resources can help Life Path 8 individuals gain a clearer understanding of their inherent qualities and how they align with their life purpose. Assessments focused on leadership, creativity, and emotional intelligence are particularly beneficial, as they resonate with the core traits of Life Path 8. By taking the time to explore these tools, individuals can create a comprehensive profile of their strengths, which can be instrumental in guiding their decisions in career, relationships, and personal growth.

As Life Path 8 individuals identify their strengths, it is essential to align these qualities with their goals and aspirations. This alignment not only enhances their effectiveness in leadership roles but also fosters a sense of fulfillment in their personal lives. By leveraging their strengths, such as financial acumen or innovative thinking, they can create opportunities for themselves and others. Moreover, recognizing their strengths allows them to build resilience against challenges, as they can draw upon these qualities in times of adversity.

Ultimately, the process of identifying personal strengths is a transformative journey for Life Path 8 individuals. It equips them with the self-awareness needed to navigate the complexities of life, from career advancement to relationship dynamics. By embracing their unique attributes and integrating them into their daily lives, they can unlock their potential and create a lasting legacy. This deep understanding of themselves not only propels them toward success but also encourages spiritual growth and development, enriching their overall life experience.

Setting Goals for Success

Setting goals for success is a fundamental practice for individuals on Life Path 8, whose journey is characterized by ambition, leadership, and a desire for achievement. To harness the potent energies of this life path, it is crucial to set clear, measurable, and attainable goals that align with both personal values and the broader aspirations of financial mastery and leadership. When Life Path 8 individuals establish goals, they create a roadmap that guides their actions and decisions, facilitating focus and momentum in their pursuits.

One effective approach to goal setting is the SMART criteria: Specific, Measurable, Achievable, Relevant, and Time-bound. For Life Path 8 personalities, this method provides a structured framework that can enhance clarity and increase the likelihood of success. For instance, rather than stating a vague desire to improve financial stability, a Life Path 8 individual might set a specific goal to save a certain percentage of their income over the next year. This specificity not only fosters accountability but also enables them to track progress effectively, reinforcing motivation as milestones are reached.

Additionally, it is important for Life Path 8 individuals to consider both short-term and long-term goals. Short-term goals can serve as stepping stones toward achieving larger aspirations, such as career advancement or building a legacy. By breaking down significant ambitions into smaller, manageable tasks, Life Path 8 individuals can maintain a sense of accomplishment and direction. This approach mitigates feelings of overwhelm and allows for a more systematic pursuit of success, whether that pertains to financial mastery, health, or personal development.

Moreover, aligning goals with personal values is essential for sustaining motivation and commitment. Life Path 8 individuals often possess strong leadership qualities and a desire to make an impact. Therefore, setting goals that resonate with their core beliefs—such as promoting financial literacy or contributing to community well-being—will not only enhance their personal satisfaction but also amplify their influence as leaders. This alignment ensures that the journey toward achieving these goals is fulfilling and meaningful.

Finally, regular evaluation and adjustment of goals are crucial for ongoing success. Life Path 8 individuals may encounter unique challenges that require flexibility and adaptation. By routinely assessing their progress and remaining open to recalibrating their goals, they can respond effectively to changing circumstances and maintain their trajectory toward success. This proactive approach empowers Life Path 8 individuals to navigate obstacles with resilience and creativity, ultimately reinforcing their capacity to unlock their full potential and thrive in all aspects of life.

Embracing Leadership Qualities

Embracing leadership qualities is essential for individuals on the Life Path 8 journey, as they are inherently positioned to take charge and influence others positively. Life Path 8 individuals often possess a natural drive for success and an affinity for authority, which can manifest as strong leadership capabilities. Understanding these qualities and how to cultivate them further enables Life Path 8 personalities to unlock their full potential. By honing their leadership skills, they can navigate challenges, inspire others, and create impactful legacies.

Effective communication is a cornerstone of strong leadership, and Life Path 8 individuals must prioritize developing this skill. Clear, assertive, and empathetic communication fosters trust and respect among team members, making it easier to lead with confidence. Life Path 8 personalities should focus on actively listening to others, valuing their input, and being open to different perspectives. This not only enhances collaboration but also strengthens relationships, a crucial aspect of any leadership role, whether in business or personal interactions.

Another vital leadership quality for Life Path 8 individuals is resilience. The path is often riddled with obstacles and challenges, requiring a steadfast spirit and the ability to rebound from setbacks. Life Path 8 personalities can embrace resilience by maintaining a positive mindset, learning from failures, and remaining adaptable in the face of change. This perseverance not only sets a powerful example for others but also solidifies their position as trusted leaders who can guide their teams through difficult times.

Visionary thinking is also critical for those on the Life Path 8. Effective leaders must possess the ability to envision future possibilities and create strategic plans to achieve those goals. Life Path 8 individuals are often drawn to ambitious projects and innovative solutions, making it essential for them to harness this visionary quality. By setting clear, achievable objectives and inspiring others to work toward a shared vision, they can drive collective success and foster an environment that encourages creativity and forward-thinking.

Lastly, the importance of ethical leadership cannot be overstated. Life Path 8 personalities have the potential to wield significant influence, and with that power comes the responsibility to act with integrity and fairness. Embracing ethical leadership involves making decisions that prioritize the well-being of all stakeholders and fostering a culture of accountability. By exemplifying strong moral principles, Life Path 8 individuals can build enduring trust and respect, ensuring that their leadership not only drives success but also contributes positively to their communities and legacies.

Chapter 3

Financial Mastery for Life Path 8 Individuals

Understanding Financial Independence

Financial independence is a concept that resonates deeply with individuals on the Life Path 8 journey. It embodies the freedom to make choices aligned with one's values and aspirations, unburdened by financial constraints. For Life Path 8 individuals, who often possess a strong drive for success and a natural inclination towards leadership, understanding financial independence is not just about accumulating wealth; it is about harnessing that wealth to create a meaningful and impactful life. This understanding requires a comprehensive approach that integrates financial literacy, strategic planning, and personal values.

At its core, financial independence involves more than just having enough money to cover expenses; it signifies the ability to generate income and build assets that provide security and opportunities. Life Path 8 individuals are typically ambitious and goal-oriented, qualities that can be leveraged to achieve financial stability. By setting clear financial goals and developing a plan to reach those objectives, they can foster a sense of control over their financial destiny. This process encourages the cultivation of skills such as budgeting, investing, and understanding the nuances of cash flow management.

Leadership strategies play a pivotal role in attaining financial independence for Life Path 8 individuals. Their innate leadership abilities can be harnessed to guide teams, influence decision-making, and create innovative solutions to financial challenges. By applying these strategies in both personal and professional contexts, they can inspire others while simultaneously advancing their own financial goals. Networking and collaboration become essential tools, as forming relationships with like-minded individuals can open doors to new opportunities and resources that further facilitate financial growth.

Moreover, the pursuit of financial independence demands a commitment to personal development and self-awareness. Life Path 8 individuals often face unique challenges, including the pressure to succeed and the fear of failure. Overcoming these challenges requires resilience and a mindset that embraces growth. Engaging in health and wellness practices can enhance mental clarity and emotional stability, providing a solid foundation for making sound financial decisions. Balancing ambition with well-being ensures that their pursuit of wealth does not come at the cost of personal fulfillment.

Ultimately, financial independence for Life Path 8 individuals is about building a legacy that reflects their values and aspirations. This legacy extends beyond financial wealth to encompass contributions to society and the empowerment of others. By understanding the principles of financial independence, Life Path 8 individuals can create a life of abundance that not only benefits themselves but also positively impacts their communities. Embracing this journey equips them with the tools needed to master their destiny, aligning their financial practices with their life purpose.

Investment Strategies for Growth

Investment strategies for growth are essential for individuals on Life Path 8, who often possess a natural affinity for leadership and financial mastery. These strategies not only cater to the desire for wealth accumulation but also align with the ambitious nature of Life Path 8 individuals. By understanding the principles of growth investing, you can effectively harness your inherent strengths to unlock financial opportunities that contribute to your overall life purpose.

One effective strategy is to focus on sectors that align with future trends and innovations. Life Path 8 individuals are often visionaries, able to foresee changes in the marketplace. Investing in technology, renewable energy, or healthcare can yield substantial returns. Conduct thorough research to identify companies leading these industries and evaluate their growth potential. By aligning your investments with sectors that resonate with your values and vision, you can create a portfolio that not only grows your wealth but also supports your overarching goals.

Diversification is another crucial element in growth investment strategies. Life Path 8 personalities thrive on stability and security, making it imperative to spread investments across various asset classes. This approach mitigates risks associated with market fluctuations and helps maintain a steady growth trajectory. Consider a mix of stocks, bonds, real estate, and alternative investments. Each asset class has its own strengths and weaknesses, and a well-balanced portfolio can withstand economic downturns while capitalizing on growth opportunities.

Incorporating a long-term perspective is vital for Life Path 8 individuals seeking growth. Patience is a virtue in investing, and understanding that not all investments will yield immediate returns is essential. Craft a strategy that focuses on long-term gains rather than short-term victories. This mindset aligns with the Life Path 8 tendency to build and create lasting legacies. Regularly review and adjust your portfolio, but avoid the temptation to react hastily to market volatility. Consistency and discipline are key to achieving the growth you desire.

Lastly, continuous education and self-improvement play a significant role in mastering investment strategies. Life Path 8 individuals are often lifelong learners, and staying informed about market trends, economic conditions, and investment techniques is crucial. Attend workshops, read financial literature, and seek mentorship from experienced investors. By committing to personal growth in your investment knowledge, you will enhance your ability to make informed decisions that align with your financial goals and overall aspirations as a Life Path 8 individual.

Creating Multiple Income Streams

Creating multiple income streams is a crucial strategy for Life Path 8 individuals, who often seek financial mastery and stability. As natural leaders and ambitious achievers, Life Path 8 personalities thrive on the pursuit of success in various aspects of life, including their financial endeavors. Establishing diverse income sources not only enhances financial security but also aligns with the Life Path 8's innate ability to manage resources effectively. By diversifying income, you can leverage your skills and knowledge in multiple areas, thereby creating a more robust financial foundation.

To begin creating multiple income streams, it is essential first to assess your existing skills, interests, and resources. Life Path 8 individuals often possess strong leadership abilities, entrepreneurial spirit, and a keen understanding of business dynamics. Identify areas where you excel and consider how these can translate into additional income opportunities. This might include starting a side business, investing in real estate, or offering consulting services in your field of expertise. Regularly evaluating your strengths can lead to innovative ideas that can be monetized effectively.

Investing is another powerful avenue for generating income streams. Life Path 8 individuals are typically comfortable with financial risks and can effectively analyze market trends. Explore different investment vehicles such as stocks, bonds, or mutual funds, and develop a diversified portfolio that aligns with your financial goals. Additionally, consider passive income options like dividend stocks or rental properties. The key is to conduct thorough research and stay informed about market fluctuations, ensuring that your investments yield sustainable returns over time.

Another strategy for creating multiple income streams is to embrace technology and the digital economy. The rise of online platforms offers numerous opportunities for Life Path 8 individuals to monetize their skills and knowledge. From e-commerce to digital marketing, the internet provides a vast landscape for entrepreneurial pursuits. Consider creating online courses, writing e-books, or launching a blog that shares your expertise. Engaging in these activities not only generates income but also enhances your reputation as a leader in your niche, further solidifying your legacy as a Life Path 8 individual.

Finally, networking and establishing partnerships can amplify your efforts in creating multiple income streams. Life Path 8 personalities excel in building relationships and can leverage their connections to explore collaborative opportunities. Attend industry events, join professional organizations, or engage in online communities related to your interests. By fostering relationships with like-minded individuals, you can discover new avenues for income generation, share resources, and gather valuable insights. Building a supportive network is essential in navigating the complexities of financial mastery and can lead to unexpected opportunities that enrich your journey as a Life Path 8 individual.

Chapter 4

Leadership Strategies for Life Path 8

Developing Effective Leadership Skills

Developing effective leadership skills is crucial for individuals on Life Path 8, as it aligns with their inherent strengths and drive for success. Life Path 8 individuals are often characterized by their ambition, resilience, and a strong desire to achieve their goals. To cultivate leadership skills, it is essential for them to harness these traits while also focusing on emotional intelligence, communication, and the ability to inspire others. By understanding the dynamics of effective leadership, Life Path 8 individuals can create a lasting impact in their personal and professional lives.

One of the foundational elements of effective leadership for Life Path 8 individuals is self-awareness. Recognizing their own strengths, weaknesses, and emotional triggers allows them to navigate challenges with confidence. Self-awareness also enhances their ability to empathize with others, fostering stronger relationships and collaboration within teams. Life Path 8 individuals should regularly reflect on their experiences and seek feedback from peers to develop a more profound understanding of their leadership style and its impact on others.

Communication plays a pivotal role in leadership effectiveness. Life Path 8 individuals must master the art of clear and persuasive communication to articulate their vision and motivate those around them. This involves not only conveying messages effectively but also being an active listener. By engaging in open dialogues and valuing input from team members, Life Path 8 leaders can cultivate an inclusive environment that encourages creativity and innovation. Building strong communication skills will help them navigate complex situations and reinforce their authority as leaders.

Another crucial aspect of leadership for Life Path 8 individuals is the ability to make decisive, informed decisions. Their natural inclination toward strategic thinking enables them to analyze situations critically and weigh potential outcomes. However, effective leaders also recognize the importance of adaptability and flexibility in their approach. Leadership often requires adjusting plans in response to unforeseen challenges. Life Path 8 individuals should embrace a mindset that is open to change, empowering them to lead their teams through uncertainty with confidence.

Finally, developing a vision is essential for Life Path 8 leaders. A compelling vision not only guides their decisions but also serves as a source of inspiration for others. Life Path 8 individuals should focus on creating a vision that reflects their values and aspirations while being grounded in practicality. This vision should be communicated consistently to ensure that it resonates with their teams. By embodying their vision and demonstrating commitment, Life Path 8 leaders can motivate others to work towards common goals, ultimately leaving a lasting legacy that reflects their journey and achievements.

Building and Leading Teams

Building and leading teams is a critical skill for individuals on Life Path 8, who are often drawn to leadership roles due to their inherent ambition and drive for success. To effectively build and lead teams, it is essential to recognize the unique strengths and qualities that Life Path 8 individuals possess. These include a natural ability to inspire others, a strong sense of responsibility, and a keen understanding of the importance of structure and organization. By harnessing these traits, Life Path 8 individuals can create cohesive and high-performing teams that work towards common goals.

Effective communication is the cornerstone of successful team building. Life Path 8 individuals must prioritize open and honest dialogue, ensuring that all team members feel heard and valued. This approach not only fosters trust but also encourages collaboration among diverse personalities. By establishing clear communication channels and promoting a culture of feedback, leaders can empower their teams to express ideas and concerns freely. This inclusive environment ultimately leads to enhanced problem-solving and innovation, aligning with the Life Path 8's goal of achieving excellence.

Moreover, understanding individual team members' strengths and weaknesses is vital for optimizing performance. Life Path 8 leaders should take the time to assess the unique skills and motivations of each team member, allowing for strategic delegation of tasks that play to those strengths. By empowering individuals to take ownership of their roles, leaders can cultivate a sense of accountability and commitment. This tailored approach not only boosts morale but also drives productivity, as team members are more likely to excel when their talents are recognized and utilized effectively.

Conflict resolution is another crucial aspect of team leadership for Life Path 8 individuals. Given their assertive nature, they may sometimes encounter challenges in managing differing opinions or interpersonal tensions. Developing strong conflict resolution skills can mitigate these issues and transform challenges into opportunities for growth. Life Path 8 leaders should approach conflicts with a solution-oriented mindset, facilitating discussions that focus on common goals rather than personal grievances. By modeling calm and constructive behavior, leaders can guide their teams through conflicts, fostering resilience and unity.

Lastly, building a legacy as a Life Path 8 individual involves mentoring and developing future leaders within the team. By investing in the growth and development of team members, Life Path 8 leaders can extend their influence and ensure the continuity of their vision. This commitment to nurturing talent not only enhances team dynamics but also reinforces the leader's role as a catalyst for positive change. As Life Path 8 individuals embrace their leadership journey, they must remember that effective team building is not just about achieving goals; it is about uplifting others and creating a lasting impact on their lives and the community.

Navigating Conflict and Negotiation

Conflict and negotiation are integral aspects of both personal and professional life, particularly for individuals on Life Path 8. Known for their ambition, authority, and leadership qualities, Life Path 8 individuals may often find themselves in situations of disagreement or conflict. Understanding the dynamics of conflict and mastering negotiation techniques can significantly enhance their ability to navigate these challenges effectively. This not only helps in resolving disputes but also fosters stronger relationships and promotes a collaborative atmosphere in various settings.

The first step in navigating conflict is recognizing the underlying motivations and emotions of all parties involved. Life Path 8 individuals possess a natural inclination towards control and assertiveness, which can sometimes be perceived as confrontational. Acknowledging this tendency allows them to approach conflicts with a more empathetic mindset. By practicing active listening, they can uncover the real issues at stake, allowing for a more productive dialogue. This approach not only demonstrates respect for others' perspectives but also encourages a collaborative effort to find mutually beneficial solutions.

Effective negotiation requires a balance between assertiveness and flexibility. Life Path 8 individuals often excel in setting clear goals and outlining their expectations. However, the key to successful negotiation lies in the ability to adapt and compromise when necessary. Embracing a mindset of collaboration rather than competition can lead to more favorable outcomes. By focusing on shared interests and common ground, Life Path 8 individuals can transform potential conflicts into opportunities for partnership and growth, thereby enhancing their leadership effectiveness.

Additionally, honing emotional intelligence is crucial for Life Path 8 individuals during conflict resolution. Being aware of one's own emotional triggers and biases can prevent escalation and promote calmness in tense situations. Developing skills such as empathy, self-regulation, and effective communication can empower Life Path 8 individuals to navigate conflicts with grace and confidence. This emotional acumen not only aids in resolving disputes but also cultivates a reputation for being a fair and respected leader.

Lastly, viewing conflict as a natural part of growth can shift the perspective of Life Path 8 individuals from one of avoidance to one of proactive engagement. By embracing challenges as opportunities to refine their negotiation skills and strengthen their relationships, they can cultivate a legacy of resilience and innovation. As they learn to navigate conflicts with poise and purpose, Life Path 8 individuals not only unlock their potential but also inspire others to do the same, ultimately elevating their personal and professional journeys.

Chapter 5

Health and Wellness for Life Path 8 Personalities

Importance of Physical Health

Physical health is a cornerstone of overall well-being, particularly for individuals aligned with Life Path 8. This path emphasizes ambition, leadership, and the pursuit of material success, but the drive for achievement can often overshadow the essential need for physical wellness. Life Path 8 individuals are typically goal-oriented and may prioritize work over self-care. However, neglecting physical health can lead to burnout, diminished productivity, and ultimately hinder the potential for success. Recognizing the importance of maintaining a healthy body is crucial to sustaining the energy required for achieving the high aspirations characteristic of this life path.

Moreover, physical health directly influences mental clarity and emotional stability, both of which are vital for effective leadership. Life Path 8 individuals often find themselves in positions where decision-making and strategic thinking are paramount. Regular exercise, a balanced diet, and adequate rest contribute to enhanced cognitive function, allowing for sharper focus and quicker problem-solving abilities. Maintaining physical health establishes a foundation that supports both the mental and emotional resilience needed to navigate the challenges that come with leadership roles.

In addition to improved cognitive abilities, physical health fosters greater resilience against stress, a common experience for those on Life Path 8. The pressures of financial mastery and career advancement can lead to overwhelming stress levels if not managed properly. Engaging in physical activities can serve as a powerful outlet for stress relief, allowing individuals to recharge and refocus. Incorporating exercise into daily routines not only promotes better physical health but also cultivates a healthier mindset, which is essential for overcoming the unique challenges faced by Life Path 8 personalities.

Furthermore, the importance of physical health is not limited to the individual; it extends to relationships and teamwork. Life Path 8 individuals often find themselves in leadership positions that require collaboration and effective communication. A healthy individual is better equipped to engage with others positively and productively. By prioritizing physical wellness, Life Path 8 personalities can inspire those around them, fostering a culture of health and vitality within their teams and personal relationships. This holistic approach not only benefits individual well-being but also enhances overall group dynamics.

Lastly, embracing physical health as a priority can significantly contribute to legacy building, a core aspect of Life Path 8. Individuals on this path are often driven by a desire to leave a lasting impact. A commitment to physical wellness not only ensures longevity but also sets an example for future generations. By integrating health and wellness into their lifestyle, Life Path 8 individuals can create a legacy that encompasses not only financial achievements but also a testament to the importance of holistic health, thereby unlocking their full potential and influencing others to do the same.

Mental Well-Being and Stress Management

Mental well-being is a critical component for individuals on Life Path 8, who often find themselves navigating high-stakes environments characterized by ambition, leadership, and financial aspirations. Given the inherent challenges associated with this path, such as the pressure to succeed and the weight of responsibility, effective stress management becomes essential. Life Path 8 individuals are natural leaders who thrive on overcoming obstacles, yet they must also cultivate resilience and emotional stability to maintain their overall well-being. Developing strategies to manage stress will not only enhance their personal lives but will also positively influence their professional endeavors and relationships.

One effective approach to stress management is the practice of mindfulness and meditation. Life Path 8 individuals can benefit significantly from dedicating time each day to quiet reflection and mental clarity. Engaging in mindfulness helps to center the mind, allowing for a clearer perspective on challenges and decisions. This practice fosters emotional regulation, enabling Life Path 8 individuals to respond to stressors with a calm and focused mindset. Incorporating meditation into a daily routine can lead to improved concentration, reduced anxiety, and enhanced emotional resilience, all of which are vital for navigating the complexities of leadership and financial management.

Physical well-being also plays a pivotal role in mental health. Life Path 8 personalities often lead busy lives, juggling multiple responsibilities and striving for success. However, neglecting physical health can exacerbate stress and hinder overall performance. Regular exercise, a balanced diet, and sufficient sleep are foundational elements that contribute to mental well-being. Engaging in physical activities not only promotes fitness but also releases endorphins, which elevate mood and reduce stress. Life Path 8 individuals should prioritize self-care routines that incorporate these elements, ensuring they maintain the energy and vitality needed to pursue their goals effectively.

Another vital aspect of stress management is the cultivation of a supportive network. Life Path 8 individuals often carry the burden of leadership, but they should not hesitate to seek support from friends, family, or professional mentors. Establishing connections with like-minded individuals who understand the unique challenges of this path can provide emotional support and valuable insights. Open communication within these relationships fosters a sense of belonging and reduces feelings of isolation, which can be particularly beneficial during times of stress. Moreover, sharing experiences and strategies with peers can lead to collaborative solutions and innovative approaches to common challenges.

Lastly, developing a proactive approach to stress management is essential for Life Path 8 individuals. This involves recognizing the early signs of stress and implementing strategies to mitigate its impact before it escalates. Creating a structured schedule that includes time for relaxation and downtime can help maintain balance. Additionally, setting realistic goals and breaking tasks into manageable steps can prevent overwhelm. By embracing a proactive mindset, Life Path 8 individuals can transform potential stressors into opportunities for growth and development, ultimately enhancing their journey toward mastering their destiny.

Holistic Approaches to Wellness

Holistic approaches to wellness involve integrating various aspects of life to achieve a balanced and harmonious existence, particularly for individuals on the Life Path 8 journey. Life Path 8 individuals are often characterized by their strong leadership qualities, ambition, and drive for financial success. However, this relentless pursuit can sometimes lead to imbalances, making it essential to adopt holistic practices that nurture not just financial and career aspirations but also physical, emotional, and spiritual well-being. By embracing a holistic perspective, Life Path 8 individuals can unlock their full potential and create a more fulfilling life.

Physical wellness is a cornerstone of a holistic approach. For Life Path 8 individuals, focusing on regular exercise, proper nutrition, and adequate rest can significantly enhance their energy levels and overall productivity. Engaging in physical activities such as yoga or martial arts not only strengthens the body but also cultivates discipline and focus, which are vital traits for leaders. Additionally, incorporating mindfulness practices, such as meditation, can help clear the mind and reduce stress, allowing for better decision-making in both personal and professional realms.

Emotional wellness is equally important for Life Path 8 individuals, who may often find themselves overwhelmed by their ambitions and responsibilities. Understanding and managing emotions through practices like journaling or therapy can provide valuable insights into one's emotional landscape. Building strong support networks is also crucial; surrounding oneself with positive influences can foster resilience and emotional stability. By prioritizing emotional health, Life Path 8 individuals can maintain the motivation needed to pursue their goals while ensuring they do not neglect their inner well-being.

Spiritual growth plays a significant role in the holistic wellness framework. Life Path 8 individuals can benefit from exploring their spiritual beliefs and practices, whether through meditation, mindfulness, or connecting with nature. This exploration can lead to a deeper understanding of their life purpose and aspirations, aligning their ambitions with a sense of higher meaning. Engaging in spiritual practices not only enhances self-awareness but also encourages a sense of gratitude, which can transform challenges into opportunities for growth.

Finally, integrating all these aspects of wellness into daily life requires effective time management and prioritization, skills that Life Path 8 individuals are already familiar with. Developing a structured routine that allocates time for physical activity, emotional reflection, and spiritual practices can create a balanced lifestyle. By consciously setting aside time for wellness, Life Path 8 individuals can cultivate resilience and clarity in their pursuits, ultimately leading to a more impactful and legacy-driven existence. Embracing a holistic approach to wellness empowers Life Path 8 individuals to thrive on all fronts, harmonizing their ambitions with a fulfilling and balanced life.

Chapter 6

Spiritual Growth and Development for Life Path 8

Exploring Spiritual Beliefs

Exploring spiritual beliefs is a pivotal aspect of understanding the complexities inherent in Life Path 8 individuals. This life path is often associated with power, ambition, and a strong drive for success, yet beneath this exterior lies a profound spiritual journey that can significantly influence personal and professional outcomes. For those on this path, integrating spiritual beliefs into their daily lives can provide a deeper sense of purpose and a framework for navigating the challenges that arise in the pursuit of financial mastery and leadership.

Life Path 8 individuals are frequently driven by material success and personal achievement. However, spirituality can serve as a grounding force that helps to balance these ambitions. Many Life Path 8 individuals may find themselves drawn to philosophies that emphasize abundance, such as the Law of Attraction, which aligns well with their goals. By understanding how spiritual principles interact with their ambitions, they can harness these beliefs to promote not only financial success but also a more holistic approach to life that includes health, wellness, and personal fulfillment.

As leaders, Life Path 8 individuals often face unique challenges in their relationships and career advancement. Exploring spiritual beliefs can enhance their leadership strategies by fostering empathy, intuition, and a deeper connection with others. Spirituality encourages a sense of community and collaboration, which can be particularly beneficial for Life Path 8 individuals who may sometimes struggle with isolation due to their intense focus on goals. By integrating spiritual practices such as mindfulness or meditation, they can cultivate a leadership style that is both assertive and compassionate, allowing them to inspire and motivate others effectively.

The journey of spiritual growth and development is not without its hurdles. Life Path 8 individuals may encounter skepticism or resistance from those around them when expressing their spiritual beliefs. This can lead to challenges in personal relationships, where misunderstandings about spiritual priorities may arise. It is crucial for Life Path 8 individuals to remain steadfast in their beliefs and to communicate openly with their partners, friends, and colleagues. By articulating how their spirituality enhances their ambition and drives their success, they can create a supportive environment that acknowledges both their material and spiritual aspirations.

Ultimately, exploring spiritual beliefs is essential for Life Path 8 individuals seeking to build a lasting legacy. Their quest for financial mastery and leadership can be enriched by a solid spiritual foundation that guides their decisions and actions. By recognizing the interplay between their ambitions and their spiritual values, they can create a life that not only achieves success but also resonates with their inner truth. This holistic approach fosters a legacy that transcends mere financial accomplishments, leaving behind a transformative impact on their communities and the world at large.

Practices for Inner Peace

Practices for inner peace are essential for individuals on Life Path 8, as they often navigate the complexities of ambition, financial mastery, and leadership. Life Path 8 personalities are driven by their goals and the pursuit of success, which can lead to stress and overwhelm if not balanced with practices that cultivate tranquility. By integrating specific techniques into daily routines, Life Path 8 individuals can create a harmonious alignment between their aspirations and their inner selves, fostering resilience and clarity.

Mindfulness meditation stands out as a powerful practice for achieving inner peace. This technique encourages individuals to focus on their breath and remain present in the moment, allowing for a break from the relentless pursuit of goals. For Life Path 8 individuals, who may have a tendency to ruminate on past failures or future ambitions, mindfulness helps cultivate a sense of acceptance and serenity. Establishing a daily meditation practice, even for just a few minutes, can significantly enhance emotional regulation and decrease anxiety, enabling clearer decision-making in both personal and professional realms.

In addition to mindfulness, engaging in physical activities tailored to personal preferences can greatly enhance inner peace. Life Path 8 individuals often thrive in leadership roles, but the demands of such positions can lead to physical and mental fatigue. Incorporating practices like yoga, tai chi, or even regular walks in nature can provide a much-needed outlet for stress and a way to reconnect with the body. These activities not only promote physical health but also allow for a deeper connection to one's inner self, fostering a balanced approach to the often chaotic environment that Life Path 8 individuals navigate.

Cultivating gratitude is another essential practice that can shift perspectives and enhance inner peace. Life Path 8 individuals are often focused on achieving more, which can sometimes lead to a sense of dissatisfaction with the present. By intentionally practicing gratitude—whether through journaling or simply reflecting on daily blessings— Life Path 8 personalities can cultivate a more positive mindset. This practice helps in recognizing the abundance already present in their lives, fostering contentment and reducing the pressure to constantly pursue external validation or success.

Finally, establishing a supportive network of relationships plays a critical role in nurturing inner peace. Life Path 8 individuals may often find themselves in competitive environments, which can lead to feelings of isolation. Building connections with like-minded individuals who understand the unique challenges and aspirations of Life Path 8 can provide emotional support and encouragement. These relationships can serve as a safe space for sharing experiences, celebrating successes, and discussing challenges, thereby reinforcing a sense of belonging and community that is vital for maintaining inner peace amidst the pursuit of greatness.

Balancing Material and Spiritual Aspirations

Balancing material and spiritual aspirations is a critical aspect of the journey for individuals on Life Path 8. This path is often characterized by a strong drive for success, power, and financial stability. However, the challenge lies in harmonizing these material pursuits with profound spiritual growth. Life Path 8 individuals must recognize that while ambition can lead to external achievements, it is essential to nurture the inner self for a fulfilling and well-rounded life. This balance not only enriches personal well-being but also enhances the capacity to lead and inspire others.

Material success can be a double-edged sword for Life Path 8 personalities. On one hand, the drive for achievement can lead to significant financial rewards and a powerful presence in the professional realm. Yet, the relentless pursuit of material wealth can create a void if it overshadows the spiritual aspects of life. To foster a holistic approach, individuals must establish a clear vision that integrates both their material goals and spiritual aspirations. This vision serves as a roadmap, guiding actions and decisions that align with their true purpose while ensuring that financial pursuits do not eclipse the importance of inner fulfillment.

Spiritual growth for Life Path 8 individuals often involves exploring deeper questions about purpose, connection, and legacy. Engaging in practices such as meditation, mindfulness, or self-reflection can provide valuable insights that help maintain this balance. By dedicating time to spiritual development, Life Path 8 individuals can cultivate a sense of inner peace and purpose that complements their material goals. This alignment allows for a more profound connection to oneself and others, fostering healthier relationships and promoting a supportive environment where both personal and communal growth can thrive.

Furthermore, leadership strategies for Life Path 8 can benefit greatly from this balance. A leader who embodies both material success and spiritual wisdom is more likely to inspire and motivate others. When individuals on this path embrace their spiritual side, they become more empathetic, understanding, and visionary. This holistic approach to leadership not only enhances their effectiveness in guiding teams and organizations but also fosters an environment where innovation and creativity can flourish. Such leaders are often seen as pillars of strength, capable of navigating challenges while remaining grounded in their values and principles.

Ultimately, building a legacy as a Life Path 8 individual requires a conscious effort to balance material and spiritual aspirations. This balance is not merely about achieving success in one area of life but rather about creating a harmonious existence that honors both the tangible and intangible aspects of being. By prioritizing spiritual growth alongside financial mastery and leadership, Life Path 8 individuals can leave a lasting impact that transcends material wealth. They can build a legacy rooted in authenticity, purpose, and compassion, inspiring future generations to pursue a similar path of balance and fulfillment.

Chapter 7

Career Advancement Tips for Life Path 8

Identifying Career Pathways

Identifying career pathways for individuals with a Life Path 8 numerology is essential for harnessing their inherent strengths and talents. Life Path 8 individuals are often characterized by their drive, ambition, and desire for financial success. They thrive in environments where they can take charge, demonstrate leadership, and create structures that lead to tangible results. By understanding their unique attributes, Life Path 8 individuals can better align their career choices with their natural inclinations, ultimately leading to greater fulfillment and success.

When exploring career options, Life Path 8 individuals should consider fields that allow for both leadership opportunities and financial growth. Professions in management, finance, and entrepreneurship resonate particularly well with these individuals. The strategic mindset of a Life Path 8 enables them to analyze situations critically and make informed decisions that propel them forward. Additionally, roles in consulting or coaching can be highly rewarding, as they allow Life Path 8 individuals to share their expertise and empower others to achieve their potential.

It is crucial for Life Path 8 individuals to engage in self-reflection when identifying their ideal career pathways. They should assess their skills, interests, and values to determine what truly drives their passion. Taking time for introspection can help clarify whether they seek stability within established organizations or the freedom of self-employment. By aligning their career choices with personal values, Life Path 8 individuals can find paths that not only promise financial stability but also resonate with their deeper aspirations.

Networking plays a vital role in the career advancement of Life Path 8 individuals. Building relationships with like-minded professionals can open doors to new opportunities and collaborations that may not be readily apparent. Engaging in mentorship—either as a mentor or mentee—can provide valuable insights and guidance. Life Path 8 individuals should actively seek out communities and organizations that align with their career interests, leveraging these connections to further their professional growth.

In conclusion, identifying career pathways for Life Path 8 individuals involves a thoughtful blend of self-awareness, strategic planning, and relationship building. By understanding their strengths and preferences, they can navigate the complexities of the professional world with confidence. Embracing their leadership qualities and financial acumen will empower Life Path 8 individuals to create meaningful careers that not only fulfill their ambitions but also contribute positively to the lives of others. This journey of career exploration ultimately leads to a legacy that reflects their unique potential and purpose.

Networking and Building Connections

Networking and building connections are essential components for individuals on Life Path 8, especially considering their inherent leadership qualities and ambition. Life Path 8 individuals often possess a natural gravitation towards authority and influence, making it crucial to cultivate relationships that can further their goals. Networking offers opportunities to exchange ideas, gain insights, and form partnerships that can lead to mutual success. By actively engaging with others, Life Path 8 individuals can enhance their visibility and establish themselves as key players within their chosen fields.

Engaging in networking requires a strategic approach, particularly for Life Path 8 individuals who may sometimes focus too heavily on personal ambition. Building authentic connections means prioritizing quality over quantity. It is important to seek out relationships that resonate with personal values and professional aspirations. Attending industry events, joining relevant associations, and participating in community initiatives can create a supportive network that fosters growth. Life Path 8 individuals should also consider mentorship opportunities, both as mentors and mentees, to enhance their understanding and navigate complex professional landscapes.

In addition to traditional networking methods, leveraging digital platforms plays a significant role in expanding one's reach. Life Path 8 individuals should utilize social media and professional networking sites to connect with like-minded professionals and industry leaders. Sharing insights, engaging in discussions, and showcasing expertise online can attract valuable connections and open doors to new opportunities. Consistency in online presence is key, as it reinforces credibility and positions Life Path 8 individuals as thought leaders in their areas of interest.

Effective communication is a cornerstone of successful networking. Life Path 8 individuals should focus on honing their interpersonal skills to foster genuine connections. Active listening, empathy, and the ability to articulate thoughts clearly will enhance interactions and ensure that relationships are built on trust and mutual respect. Moreover, following up after initial meetings and maintaining relationships through continued engagement will solidify connections and open avenues for collaboration.

Ultimately, networking for Life Path 8 individuals is not merely about amassing contacts; it is about creating a community that reflects shared ambitions and values. By investing time and effort into building meaningful connections, Life Path 8 individuals can enhance their influence and navigate their paths toward financial mastery, leadership, and legacy creation. Through strategic networking, they can unlock potential not only for themselves but also for others, reinforcing their role as catalysts for change and innovation within their spheres of influence.

Continuous Learning and Skill Development

Continuous learning and skill development are vital components for individuals on Life Path 8, who are naturally inclined toward leadership and financial mastery. In the pursuit of their goals, Life Path 8 individuals often find themselves in competitive environments where the ability to adapt and grow can set them apart. Embracing a mindset of continuous improvement not only enhances their existing skills but also opens new avenues for personal and professional development. This ongoing commitment to learning helps Life Path 8 individuals stay relevant in their fields and equips them to tackle challenges with confidence and creativity.

One effective approach to continuous learning is the establishment of a structured plan that focuses on both short-term and long-term goals. Life Path 8 individuals can benefit from identifying specific skills that align with their career aspirations, such as financial analysis, leadership communication, or project management. By enrolling in targeted workshops, online courses, or certification programs, they can gain valuable knowledge and credentials that enhance their expertise. Furthermore, setting aside regular time for self-study allows them to explore topics of interest at their own pace, fostering a deeper understanding of their chosen subjects.

Networking and mentorship are also crucial elements in the skill development journey for Life Path 8 individuals. Engaging with peers and industry leaders can provide fresh perspectives and insights that enrich their learning experience. Participating in professional associations or attending conferences can facilitate connections that may lead to mentorship opportunities. A mentor can offer guidance, share experiences, and provide constructive feedback, helping Life Path 8 individuals navigate their career paths more effectively. This exchange of knowledge and support can be instrumental in honing their leadership skills and enhancing their ability to inspire others.

Moreover, fostering a culture of innovation and creativity is essential for Life Path 8 individuals who aspire to leave a lasting legacy. Embracing new technologies and methodologies can significantly improve efficiency and effectiveness in their endeavors. Life Path 8 individuals should remain open to experimenting with different approaches, as this willingness to innovate can lead to breakthroughs that propel them forward. Engaging in activities that stimulate creativity, such as brainstorming sessions or collaborative projects, encourages the development of new ideas and solutions that align with their visionary goals.

Lastly, it is important for Life Path 8 individuals to recognize that continuous learning is not solely an intellectual pursuit; it also encompasses emotional and spiritual growth. Engaging in practices such as mindfulness, meditation, or journaling can enhance self-awareness and emotional intelligence, which are crucial for effective leadership. By nurturing their inner selves, Life Path 8 individuals can cultivate resilience and adaptability, allowing them to thrive in the face of adversity. This holistic approach to learning and development ensures that they not only achieve their goals but also contribute positively to the lives of those around them, ultimately building a legacy that reflects their values and aspirations.

Chapter 8

Relationship Dynamics for Life Path 8

Understanding Interpersonal Relationships

Interpersonal relationships play a pivotal role in the journey of Life Path 8 individuals, as these connections significantly influence personal and professional growth. Understanding the dynamics of these relationships is essential for those on this path, as it can directly impact their ability to achieve financial mastery and assertive leadership. Life Path 8 individuals are often driven, ambitious, and goal-oriented, which can sometimes lead to misunderstandings or conflicts in relationships. Acknowledging these traits and learning to navigate them effectively can transform potential challenges into opportunities for deeper connection and mutual growth.

One key aspect of interpersonal relationships for Life Path 8 individuals is the balance between assertiveness and empathy. While being assertive is crucial for leadership and achieving goals, it is equally important to develop empathy towards others. This balance fosters healthier interactions and encourages collaboration rather than competition. Life

Path 8 individuals can benefit from honing their listening skills and practicing patience, allowing them to understand others' perspectives and needs better. By cultivating empathy, they can create stronger bonds and inspire those around them, enhancing their influence as leaders.

Trust is another fundamental element in the relationships of Life Path 8 individuals. Establishing and maintaining trust requires consistent communication and demonstrated integrity. Life Path 8 individuals are often seen as authoritative figures, and it is essential for them to model trustworthiness in their behavior. This means being honest about intentions and following through on commitments. By doing so, they not only strengthen existing relationships but also attract new connections that are aligned with their values and aspirations.

Conflict resolution is a vital skill for Life Path 8 individuals to master, as their strong personalities can sometimes lead to disagreements. Understanding that conflict is a natural part of any relationship can help them approach these situations with a constructive mindset. Employing effective communication strategies, such as using "I" statements and focusing on solutions rather than blame, can lead to more productive discussions. Embracing conflict as an opportunity for growth and understanding can enhance relationships and foster a more supportive network.

Finally, recognizing the importance of personal boundaries is crucial for Life Path 8 individuals. These boundaries help maintain a sense of self while engaging with others, ensuring that relationships are healthy and mutually beneficial.

Learning to say no when necessary and prioritizing personal needs can prevent feelings of overwhelm and resentment. By establishing clear boundaries, Life Path 8 individuals can create space for deeper connections and more meaningful interactions, ultimately contributing to their overall well-being and success in both personal and professional realms.

Building Healthy Partnerships

Building healthy partnerships is essential for Life Path 8 individuals, as these relationships significantly influence their financial success, leadership potential, and overall well-being. Life Path 8s are naturally driven and ambitious, often setting high standards for themselves and those around them. To harness their strengths, it is vital that they engage in partnerships that foster mutual respect, understanding, and collaboration. By focusing on creating healthy dynamics, Life Path 8s can unlock their potential and create lasting legacies.

A foundational aspect of building healthy partnerships is open and effective communication. Life Path 8 individuals must practice transparency in their interactions, sharing their thoughts and feelings while also being receptive to the perspectives of others. This two-way communication fosters trust and helps to align goals, whether in business collaborations, friendships, or romantic relationships. By actively listening and valuing the input of their partners, Life Path 8s can cultivate an environment where everyone feels empowered to contribute, enhancing creativity and innovation.

Moreover, recognizing the complementary qualities of partners can enhance the strength of these relationships. Life Path 8 individuals often possess leadership qualities and a strong drive for success, which can sometimes overshadow the contributions of others. Embracing diversity in skills and perspectives allows Life Path 8s to leverage the strengths of their partners, creating a balanced and dynamic partnership. This approach not only leads to better decision-making but also helps in overcoming challenges more effectively, as different viewpoints can provide innovative solutions.

Setting clear boundaries is another crucial element in fostering healthy partnerships. Life Path 8s must understand the importance of maintaining their own identity within a relationship while also respecting the autonomy of their partners. Establishing boundaries ensures that each individual can thrive, reducing the likelihood of conflict and resentment. By discussing expectations and limitations openly, Life Path 8s can create a safe space where both parties feel valued and understood, paving the way for productive collaboration.

Lastly, nurturing partnerships requires ongoing effort and commitment. Life Path 8 individuals should prioritize regular check-ins to assess the health of their relationships, celebrating successes and addressing challenges as they arise. This proactive approach not only strengthens the bond but also reinforces a shared vision for the future. By investing time and energy into their partnerships, Life Path 8s will not only enhance their personal and professional lives but also leave a lasting impact on the world around them.

Navigating Family and Social Dynamics

Navigating family and social dynamics is a crucial aspect for individuals on Life Path 8, as their strong drive for success and leadership can often create tension in personal relationships. These individuals are naturally ambitious and goal-oriented, which can lead to a perceived imbalance between their personal aspirations and the needs of family and friends. Understanding how to balance these dynamics is essential for Life Path 8 individuals to foster harmonious relationships while pursuing their objectives.

In family settings, Life Path 8 individuals may struggle with the expectations of others, particularly if they are perceived as the primary breadwinners or leaders within the household. This can result in feelings of isolation or overwhelm, as they juggle their responsibilities. It is important for Life Path 8 individuals to communicate openly with family members about their goals and ambitions. By fostering an environment of transparency and mutual support, they can cultivate a family dynamic that respects individual aspirations while reinforcing collective unity.

Social dynamics also play a significant role in the lives of Life Path 8 individuals. Their innate leadership qualities often draw others towards them, creating a network of relationships that can be both beneficial and challenging. The desire for control and recognition may lead to conflicts in friendships or professional partnerships. To navigate these complexities, it is vital for Life Path 8 individuals to practice empathy and active listening. By valuing the perspectives of others, they can create stronger bonds and avoid misunderstandings that may arise from their assertive nature.

Moreover, Life Path 8 individuals should actively seek to establish boundaries within their social circles. This is particularly important as their drive for achievement can sometimes be misconstrued as arrogance or insensitivity. By setting clear expectations about their availability and the nature of their commitments, they can prevent feelings of resentment from building up in their relationships. This approach not only protects their well-being but also fosters respect among peers, allowing for healthier interactions.

Ultimately, mastering the navigation of family and social dynamics is a continuous process for Life Path 8 individuals. By harnessing their leadership strengths while practicing compassion and communication, they can build a legacy of strong, supportive relationships. This balance not only enhances their personal lives but also empowers them to pursue their ambitions with the backing of a robust network, ensuring that they do not sacrifice their relationships in the pursuit of success.

Chapter 9

Overcoming Challenges Unique to Life Path 8

Addressing Fear of Failure

Fear of failure is a common barrier that many individuals face, particularly those on the Life Path 8 journey, where ambition and the desire for achievement are paramount. For Life Path 8 individuals, who are often driven by a strong desire for success and financial mastery, the fear of not meeting their own expectations can be paralyzing. Understanding this fear is the first step toward overcoming it. It is crucial to recognize that failure is not the opposite of success but rather a part of the journey. Embracing this perspective allows Life Path 8 personalities to reframe failure as an opportunity for growth and learning.

To address the fear of failure effectively, Life Path 8 individuals must cultivate resilience. This involves developing a mindset that views challenges as stepping stones rather than stumbling blocks. Resilience can be nurtured through self-reflection, where one can analyze past experiences of failure and extract valuable lessons. By doing so, Life Path 8 individuals can build a personal toolkit of strategies that serve them in future endeavors, enabling them to face challenges with confidence rather than dread. This shift in perspective is essential for maintaining motivation and pursuing long-term goals.

Another vital strategy for overcoming fear of failure is setting realistic and attainable goals. Life Path 8 personalities often have grand visions for their careers and lives, but when these aspirations are not broken down into manageable steps, the enormity of the task can lead to paralysis. By establishing smaller, achievable milestones, individuals can create a sense of progress and accomplishment. This not only alleviates the fear of failure but also fosters a habit of consistent action, which is critical for financial mastery and career advancement.

Support systems play a significant role in mitigating fear of failure. Life Path 8 individuals are often natural leaders, but they can also benefit from surrounding themselves with mentors, peers, and supportive networks. Engaging with others who understand the unique challenges faced by Life Path 8 individuals can provide encouragement and perspective. Sharing experiences and strategies for overcoming setbacks can create a collective resilience that empowers individuals to take calculated risks without the paralyzing fear of failing.

Finally, integrating practices that promote mental and emotional well-being can enhance the ability to confront and manage fear of failure. Activities such as mindfulness, meditation, and physical exercise can help alleviate stress and foster a positive mindset. By prioritizing health and wellness, Life Path 8 individuals can create a balanced approach to their ambitions. This holistic strategy not only equips them to face potential failures but also enables them to maintain the stamina required for long-term success. Embracing failure as an inevitable part of the journey allows Life Path 8 individuals to unlock their true potential and build a legacy that reflects their aspirations.

Managing High Expectations

Managing high expectations is a crucial aspect of navigating life as a Life Path 8 individual. Typically characterized by ambition, drive, and a desire for success, those on this path often set lofty goals for themselves. These high expectations can serve as powerful motivators, encouraging personal and professional growth. However, they can also lead to stress, burnout, and feelings of inadequacy if not managed effectively. It is essential for Life Path 8 individuals to cultivate a healthy relationship with their expectations, ensuring they propel rather than hinder their journey toward mastery and fulfillment.

One effective strategy for managing high expectations is to practice realistic goal-setting. While ambition is a defining trait of Life Path 8 individuals, setting overly ambitious goals can create unnecessary pressure. Instead, break larger objectives into smaller, achievable milestones. This approach not only makes the journey more manageable but also allows for celebrating small victories along the way. Recognizing these incremental achievements can boost motivation and reinforce a positive mindset, making the overall pursuit of larger goals feel more attainable.

Another important aspect of managing expectations involves self-awareness and reflection. Life Path 8 individuals must regularly assess their goals and the motivations behind them. Are these expectations driven by personal aspirations, societal pressures, or external validation? By identifying the root of their ambitions, individuals can align their goals with their true values and desires. This alignment fosters a sense of authenticity and purpose, reducing the likelihood of feeling overwhelmed by expectations that do not resonate with their genuine selves.

Moreover, cultivating resilience is vital for Life Path 8 individuals managing high expectations. Resilience enables individuals to navigate setbacks and challenges without losing sight of their goals. Embracing a growth mindset, where failures are viewed as opportunities for learning rather than insurmountable obstacles, can significantly enhance resilience. Life Path 8 individuals should prioritize self-care and stress management techniques, such as mindfulness, exercise, and creative outlets, to nurture their mental and emotional well-being. This focus on resilience not only helps in managing expectations but also contributes to overall career advancement and personal growth.

Finally, communication plays a key role in managing high expectations, particularly in relationships and leadership roles. Life Path 8 individuals often find themselves in positions where their expectations may influence others, whether in professional settings or personal relationships. Openly communicating goals and expectations can foster collaboration and understanding, reducing the burden of unvoiced demands. Additionally, seeking feedback from trusted peers and mentors can provide valuable insights that help recalibrate expectations. By engaging in open dialogue, Life Path 8 individuals can create a supportive environment that encourages growth while minimizing the risk of disappointment or conflict.

Coping with Criticism and Setbacks

Coping with criticism and setbacks is an essential skill for individuals on Life Path 8, known for their ambition, leadership qualities, and drive for success. As natural achievers, Life Path 8 individuals often set high standards for themselves and others. Consequently, they can be more sensitive to criticism, particularly when it comes from peers, superiors, or those they respect. Understanding that criticism is often a reflection of others' perspectives rather than an indictment of personal worth is crucial. Engaging with constructive criticism allows for personal growth and development, enabling Life Path 8 individuals to refine their skills and enhance their leadership capabilities.

Setbacks are a natural part of any journey, especially for those who are actively pursuing ambitious goals. Life Path 8 individuals may encounter various challenges, whether in their careers, financial endeavors, or personal lives. It is vital to view setbacks not as failures but as opportunities for learning and resilience. Developing a mindset that embraces challenges can empower individuals to navigate through difficulties with grace. Instead of succumbing to discouragement, Life Path 8 individuals can leverage their innate determination to analyze setbacks, identify underlying causes, and make informed adjustments to their strategies.

Another effective approach to coping with criticism and setbacks is the practice of self-reflection. Life Path 8 individuals should take time to assess their reactions to criticism and challenges. Journaling can be a powerful tool for this purpose, allowing individuals to express their thoughts and feelings, gain perspective, and track their emotional responses over time. Reflecting on past experiences can reveal patterns in how one reacts to criticism and setbacks, promoting a deeper understanding of personal triggers and responses. This awareness enables Life Path 8 individuals to cultivate emotional intelligence, which is a vital trait for effective leadership and relationship-building.

Building a supportive network is also essential for coping with criticism and setbacks. Surrounding oneself with trusted friends, mentors, and colleagues can provide a buffer against negativity and offer valuable insights during challenging times. Engaging in open conversations about experiences with criticism can help demystify the process and foster resilience. Additionally, seeking feedback from this support network can provide a more balanced view of one's strengths and areas for improvement, reinforcing the notion that constructive criticism is a crucial element of growth rather than a personal attack.

Lastly, integrating mindfulness practices into daily routines can enhance emotional resilience when facing criticism and setbacks. Techniques such as meditation, deep breathing, and visualization can help Life Path 8 individuals center themselves and maintain perspective during turbulent times. These practices encourage a state of calm that allows for thoughtful responses rather than reactive behavior. By cultivating a mindful approach, Life Path 8 individuals can develop the fortitude needed to face criticism and setbacks with confidence, ultimately transforming challenges into stepping stones toward their greater life goals.

Chapter 10

Creativity and Innovation for Life Path 8

Harnessing Creative Potential

Harnessing creative potential is a vital aspect for individuals on Life Path 8, as it intertwines with their inherent abilities to lead, innovate, and achieve financial success. Creative potential is not merely about artistic expression but encompasses the ability to think outside the box, generate innovative solutions, and approach challenges with a fresh perspective. For Life Path 8 individuals, who often possess a strong drive for achievement and a desire to make an impact, tapping into this creativity can lead to significant advancements in their careers and personal lives.

To effectively harness this creative energy, Life Path 8 individuals should first cultivate an environment that fosters innovation. This includes surrounding themselves with diverse thinkers and engaging in collaborative projects that allow for the exchange of ideas. Creating a space where brainstorming is encouraged can lead to breakthroughs that align with their goals. Additionally, allowing time for reflection and ideation without the pressure of immediate results can help in clarifying thoughts and nurturing creative insights that may otherwise remain dormant.

Moreover, integrating creative practices into daily routines can significantly enhance overall productivity. Life Path 8 individuals often thrive under structured environments, but injecting spontaneity into their schedules can yield surprising results. Activities such as journaling, mind mapping, or even engaging in hobbies unrelated to their main pursuits can stimulate creative thinking. Such practices not only provide a mental break from their rigorous goals but also allow for the subconscious to work on problems, often leading to innovative solutions when least expected.

Embracing failure as a stepping stone to success is another crucial element in harnessing creative potential. Life Path 8 individuals may sometimes fear setbacks due to their high standards and ambition. However, re-framing failure as an essential part of the creative process can encourage experimentation and risk-taking. By viewing missteps as opportunities for growth rather than obstacles, they can cultivate resilience and adaptability, essential traits for both creative exploration and leadership.

Lastly, the integration of spiritual growth into the creative process can elevate the quality and impact of the work produced by Life Path 8 individuals. Engaging in practices such as meditation or mindfulness can help clear mental clutter, allowing for greater clarity and focus. This spiritual dimension not only enhances creativity but also aligns their work with their core values, ensuring that their contributions resonate on a deeper level. Ultimately, by embracing their creative potential, Life Path 8 individuals can unlock pathways that lead to profound personal and professional fulfillment, leaving a lasting legacy in their wake.

Fostering an Innovative Mindset

Fostering an innovative mindset is crucial for individuals on Life Path 8, as it aligns with their inherent traits of ambition, leadership, and a strong desire for success. This mindset encourages them to embrace new ideas, challenge the status quo, and seek creative solutions to complex problems. Life Path 8 individuals often find themselves in positions of authority, and cultivating innovation can help them not only advance their careers but also inspire those around them. By fostering an innovative mindset, they can harness their natural resources to build a legacy that reflects their vision and values.

One effective strategy for cultivating innovation is to encourage a culture of curiosity. Life Path 8 individuals thrive on learning and growth, and fostering an environment where questions are welcomed can lead to groundbreaking ideas. This can be achieved by creating spaces for brainstorming sessions, whether in personal or professional settings, where free thinking is encouraged. Asking open-ended questions and actively seeking diverse perspectives can stimulate creative thought processes, leading to innovative solutions that may not have been considered otherwise.

Another key aspect of fostering an innovative mindset is embracing failure as a learning opportunity. Life Path 8 individuals are often driven by a desire for success and can be deterred by setbacks. However, re-framing failure as a stepping stone rather than a stumbling block is essential. Recognizing that each failure provides valuable insights allows for growth and adaptation. This resilience is a hallmark of innovative thinkers, enabling them to pivot and refine their strategies rather than give in to discouragement.

Integrating technology and new methodologies can also play a significant role in enhancing creativity and innovation. Life Path 8 individuals should stay informed about emerging trends and tools that can streamline processes and inspire fresh ideas. By leveraging these advancements, they can enhance their problem-solving capabilities and improve efficiency in their endeavors. Additionally, participating in workshops or training sessions related to creativity and innovation can provide new skills and techniques that can be applied in their professional and personal lives.

Lastly, collaboration is a vital component of fostering an innovative mindset. Life Path 8 individuals often excel in leadership roles, yet sharing the spotlight can lead to unexpected insights and innovative breakthroughs. Engaging with a diverse group of individuals, including those from different backgrounds and areas of expertise, can lead to a richer exchange of ideas. By valuing collaboration and creating networks that encourage mutual support and creative exploration, Life Path 8 individuals can truly unlock their potential and elevate their impact in their chosen paths.

Applying Creativity in Professional Settings

Creativity is often perceived as a trait reserved for artists and free spirits, but it plays a crucial role in professional settings, particularly for individuals on Life Path 8. Those on this path are known for their ambition and drive, but integrating creativity into their professional lives can enhance their effectiveness as leaders and innovators. By adopting a creative mindset, Life Path 8 individuals can unlock new strategies for financial mastery, career advancement, and even relationship dynamics within the workplace.

One of the primary benefits of applying creativity in a professional context is the ability to solve problems innovatively. Life Path 8 individuals frequently encounter challenges that require not just logical reasoning but also inventive solutions. By utilizing creative thinking, they can explore unconventional approaches to issues, whether it be in financial planning or team management. This not only leads to more effective outcomes but also fosters a culture of innovation within their organizations, encouraging team members to think outside the box.

Moreover, creativity can significantly enhance leadership strategies for those on Life Path 8. Leaders who embrace creative thinking are better equipped to inspire and motivate their teams. By encouraging open dialogue and brainstorming sessions, they create an environment where diverse ideas are valued. This inclusivity not only strengthens team cohesion but also leads to more robust and dynamic strategies that can propel the organization forward. Effective leaders understand that creativity is not just an individual endeavor but a collaborative process that can yield remarkable results.

In the realm of financial mastery, creativity can lead to novel approaches for wealth accumulation and investment. Life Path 8 individuals are often drawn to business and finance, and employing creative strategies can set them apart from competitors. This might involve exploring alternative investment avenues, developing unique marketing strategies, or leveraging technology in innovative ways. By thinking creatively, they can identify opportunities that others may overlook, ultimately enhancing their financial portfolios and securing their legacy.

Lastly, the application of creativity extends to personal well-being and relationship dynamics for Life Path 8 individuals. Engaging in creative activities can serve as a powerful stress relief, promoting overall health and wellness. Additionally, creative expression can improve communication and understanding within personal and professional relationships. By sharing ideas and collaborating on creative projects, Life Path 8 individuals can deepen connections with peers and loved ones, fostering a supportive environment that encourages growth and resilience. Thus, incorporating creativity into their professional settings not only benefits their careers but also enhances their overall quality of life.

Chapter 11

Time Management Techniques for Life Path 8

Prioritizing Tasks Effectively

Prioritizing tasks effectively is an essential skill for individuals on Life Path 8, who often find themselves navigating a complex landscape of responsibilities and ambitions. As natural leaders, Life Path 8 individuals are driven by a desire to achieve financial mastery and make a meaningful impact in their careers. To harness their innate potential, it is crucial to develop a system for prioritization that aligns with their long-term goals and values. This involves recognizing the most pressing tasks that will propel them toward success while also maintaining balance in their personal lives.

A practical approach to prioritizing tasks begins with a clear understanding of one's goals. Life Path 8 individuals should take time to articulate their short-term and long-term objectives, considering how each task contributes to these outcomes. By creating a comprehensive list of goals, they can assess which tasks are most aligned with their aspirations in areas such as career advancement, financial growth, and personal development. This clarity enables them to allocate time and resources more effectively, ensuring that their efforts are directed toward high-impact activities.

Another effective strategy is to utilize the Eisenhower Matrix, a time management tool that distinguishes between urgent and important tasks. Life Path 8 individuals can categorize their responsibilities into four quadrants: urgent and important, important but not urgent, urgent but not important, and neither urgent nor important. This visual representation allows them to identify priorities quickly, ensuring that they focus on tasks that require immediate attention while also scheduling time for important long-term projects. By regularly reviewing and adjusting their task list, they can maintain a dynamic approach to prioritization that reflects their evolving circumstances.

In addition to these techniques, it is vital for Life Path 8 individuals to recognize the importance of self-care and wellness in their prioritization process. The drive for success can often lead to neglecting personal health and well-being, which can ultimately hinder productivity and creativity. By incorporating wellness activities into their schedules, such as exercise, meditation, or leisure pursuits, Life Path 8 individuals can recharge their energy and maintain mental clarity. This holistic approach to prioritization not only enhances their performance but also fosters a sustainable lifestyle that supports their leadership aspirations.

Lastly, cultivating a support system can greatly enhance the ability to prioritize tasks. Life Path 8 individuals often thrive in collaborative environments where they can share responsibilities and gain insights from others. By surrounding themselves with like-minded individuals and mentors, they can leverage diverse perspectives and experiences to refine their prioritization strategies. This network not only provides accountability but also encourages continuous learning, allowing Life Path 8 individuals to adapt their approach as they evolve in their personal and professional journeys. Prioritizing tasks effectively is not just about managing time; it is about aligning actions with purpose and vision, ultimately leading to a legacy of achievement and fulfillment.

Tools for Enhanced Productivity

In the pursuit of enhanced productivity, Life Path 8 individuals can benefit immensely from a variety of tools designed to streamline efforts and optimize results. Understanding that their life path is often associated with ambition, leadership, and a strong drive for financial success, these tools can serve as vital instruments to harness their innate capabilities effectively. From digital applications to traditional methodologies, the right tools can transform how Life Path 8 individuals approach their goals, ensuring that they not only set high targets but also achieve them with efficiency and clarity.

Project management software is a cornerstone for enhancing productivity, enabling Life Path 8 individuals to organize tasks, set deadlines, and monitor progress seamlessly. Tools such as Trello, Asana, or Monday.com allow users to visualize their projects, breaking them down into manageable components. This approach aligns with the strategic mindset of Life Path 8 individuals, who thrive on clarity and structured planning. By employing such tools, they can delegate responsibilities effectively, track their team's contributions, and maintain a sharp focus on overarching objectives, ultimately leading to successful outcomes in their professional endeavors.

Time management techniques are equally critical for those aligned with Life Path 8. Utilizing tools like the Pomodoro Technique or time-blocking calendars can significantly enhance focus and efficiency. Life Path 8 individuals often juggle multiple responsibilities, and mastering their time is essential to prevent burnout and maintain productivity. By allocating specific time slots for tasks, they can ensure that they dedicate sufficient attention to both their professional aspirations and personal growth. Incorporating time-tracking apps can further illuminate how their time is spent, allowing for adjustments that promote a balanced, productive lifestyle.

For financial mastery, budgeting software and investment tracking tools can empower Life Path 8 individuals to take charge of their financial futures. Applications like Mint or YNAB (You Need A Budget) facilitate real-time tracking of expenses and savings, aligning perfectly with the Life Path 8's inclination toward financial acumen. By employing these tools, they can create budgets that reflect their goals, monitor investment growth, and develop strategies to build wealth. This financial clarity not only supports their ambition but also reinforces their ability to lead and create lasting legacies.

Lastly, fostering creativity and innovation is essential for Life Path 8 individuals who wish to remain ahead in their fields. Tools such as mind mapping software or collaborative brainstorming platforms can stimulate creative thinking and collaboration. Engaging with resources like Miro or MindMeister allows them to visualize their ideas and explore new concepts, paving the way for innovative solutions in their careers and personal projects. By integrating these productivity-enhancing tools into their daily routines, Life Path 8 individuals can unlock their full potential, ensuring that their ambitious pursuits are matched by effective strategies for success.

Balancing Work and Leisure

Balancing work and leisure is crucial for individuals on Life Path 8, who often possess a strong drive for success and achievement. This path is associated with ambition, authority, and a desire for financial mastery. However, the relentless pursuit of goals can lead to burnout and dissatisfaction if not managed properly. Understanding the importance of leisure as a complement to work can enhance the overall quality of life and foster greater creativity, innovation, and productivity in professional endeavors.

For Life Path 8 individuals, work often serves as a primary source of identity and fulfillment. They tend to excel in leadership roles and are highly motivated by financial success. However, it is essential to recognize that excessive focus on work can create an imbalance that negatively impacts health and relationships. To cultivate a more harmonious existence, individuals must consciously carve out time for leisure activities that bring joy and relaxation. Engaging in hobbies, spending time with loved ones, and pursuing interests outside of work can recharge the mind and body, ultimately leading to renewed vigor in professional pursuits.

Moreover, establishing boundaries between work and leisure is vital for maintaining mental and emotional well-being. Life Path 8 individuals often struggle with the tendency to overcommit, leading to stress and a sense of overwhelm. By setting clear limits on work hours and dedicating specific times for leisure, they can create a more sustainable lifestyle. This balance not only enhances personal well-being but also improves leadership effectiveness, as individuals who are well-rested and fulfilled are better equipped to inspire and motivate others.

Incorporating mindfulness practices into daily routines can also support the balance between work and leisure. Life Path 8 personalities can benefit from techniques such as meditation, yoga, or even simple breathing exercises. These practices help cultivate awareness of the present moment and encourage a more relaxed approach to both work and leisure. By integrating mindfulness, individuals can reduce stress levels, improve focus, and foster a deeper connection to their inner selves, which is essential for personal and professional growth.

Ultimately, the journey of balancing work and leisure is an ongoing process that requires intentionality and self-reflection. Life Path 8 individuals should regularly assess their commitments and ensure that their lifestyles reflect their values and aspirations. By prioritizing leisure alongside ambition, they unlock their full potential, enhance their creativity, and build a legacy that encompasses both professional achievements and personal fulfillment. This holistic approach not only leads to greater success in their careers but also enriches their lives in meaningful ways.

Chapter 12

Building a Legacy as a Life Path 8 Individual

Defining Your Legacy

Defining your legacy as a Life Path 8 individual requires a deep understanding of your unique strengths and challenges. Life Path 8 is often associated with ambition, power, and a drive for success. As you navigate your journey, it is essential to reflect on the impact you want to leave behind. This reflection involves not only your career achievements but also the contributions you make to your community and the values you instill in others. By aligning your personal and professional goals with your core values, you can create a legacy that resonates with authenticity and purpose.

Financial mastery is a significant aspect of a Life Path 8's legacy. Understanding how to manage wealth effectively can empower you to make a lasting impact. This includes not just accumulating resources but also utilizing them for the greater good. Consider how your financial decisions reflect your values and serve your community. Whether you aim to support charitable causes, promote sustainable practices, or invest in future generations, your financial legacy should align with your vision of success. This approach will not only enhance your personal fulfillment but also inspire others to adopt similar mindset shifts.

Leadership strategies play a crucial role in defining your legacy. Life Path 8 individuals often find themselves in leadership positions due to their innate ability to inspire and motivate others. To leave a lasting legacy, it is important to cultivate a leadership style that emphasizes empathy, integrity, and vision. Effective leaders create environments where others can thrive, fostering collaboration and innovation. By mentoring those around you and encouraging their growth, you contribute to a legacy that extends beyond your own accomplishments, shaping future leaders and empowering communities.

Health and wellness are integral to sustaining the energy and drive necessary for a fulfilling legacy. Life Path 8 individuals often push themselves to achieve their goals, which can lead to burnout if self-care is neglected. Defining your legacy must include a commitment to maintaining your physical, mental, and emotional well-being. This balance enables you to be present and engaged in all areas of your life. By prioritizing health, you set an example for others, demonstrating that true success encompasses well-rounded wellness. This holistic approach not only enriches your life but also influences those who look up to you.

Ultimately, defining your legacy as a Life Path 8 individual is about creating a meaningful narrative that reflects your journey and values. Embrace the challenges unique to your path, using them as opportunities for growth and learning. By focusing on financial mastery, effective leadership, health and wellness, and community impact, you can weave a legacy that inspires and uplifts others. As you move forward, remember that your legacy is not just what you achieve but how you influence the world around you. A well-defined legacy will serve as a guiding light for future generations, ensuring that your impact endures long after you are gone.

Impacting Future Generations

Life Path 8 individuals possess an inherent drive for success and a desire to make a lasting impact. This chapter focuses on how those with this life path can leverage their strengths to influence future generations positively. The combination of ambition, leadership qualities, and a strong sense of responsibility makes Life Path 8 individuals uniquely equipped to create legacies that extend beyond their own lifetimes. By harnessing their financial acumen and leadership skills, these individuals can establish frameworks and organizations that support future leaders and innovators.

Financial mastery is a crucial component for Life Path 8 individuals aiming to impact future generations. By developing sound financial practices, they can not only secure their own futures but also create opportunities for others. This includes mentoring young entrepreneurs, investing in community projects, and contributing to educational initiatives. By sharing their knowledge and experience, Life Path 8 individuals can empower others to achieve financial independence, ensuring a ripple effect that benefits society as a whole.

In addition to financial mastery, leadership strategies play a vital role in shaping future generations. Life Path 8 individuals often find themselves in positions of authority, whether in their careers or personal lives. It is essential for them to adopt inclusive leadership practices that foster collaboration and innovation. By cultivating environments where diverse voices are heard and valued, they can inspire the next generation of leaders to think critically and act compassionately. This not only enhances team dynamics but also encourages a culture of mentorship and support.

Health and wellness are also key areas where Life Path 8 individuals can influence future generations. By prioritizing their own well-being and promoting healthy lifestyle choices, they set an example for those around them. They have the ability to advocate for holistic health practices, emphasizing the importance of physical, mental, and emotional well-being. This can lead to a more resilient and balanced society, reducing the prevalence of stress-related issues and enhancing overall quality of life for future generations.

Finally, spiritual growth and development are essential for Life Path 8 individuals seeking to leave a lasting legacy. By engaging in self-reflection and personal development, they can cultivate a deeper understanding of their purpose and values. This inner work not only enriches their own lives but also serves as a guiding light for others. Encouraging practices such as mindfulness and meditation can help future generations navigate life's challenges with greater resilience and clarity. In this way, Life Path 8 individuals can create a positive and lasting impact that resonates through the ages, shaping a brighter future for all.

Creating Meaningful Contributions to Society

Creating meaningful contributions to society is a crucial aspect of the journey for individuals on Life Path 8. This path is characterized by ambition, leadership, and a desire for material success, but true fulfillment comes from leveraging these traits to make a positive impact in the world. Life Path 8 individuals possess the unique ability to turn their vision into reality, which can be harnessed to address societal challenges and uplift communities. By aligning personal goals with the greater good, they can ensure that their achievements resonate beyond mere financial success.

Financial mastery plays a significant role in how Life Path 8 individuals can contribute meaningfully. With their natural inclination towards wealth accumulation, it is essential for them to recognize that financial resources can be powerful tools for social change. By investing in charitable causes, supporting local businesses, or funding educational initiatives, they can create a ripple effect that enhances the well-being of others. Understanding the balance between personal wealth and community support will empower Life Path 8 individuals to use their financial acumen for transformative purposes.

Leadership strategies are another critical component in fostering meaningful contributions. Life Path 8 individuals are often seen as natural leaders, and they can leverage this trait to inspire and mobilize others. By championing causes that resonate with their values and engaging others in their vision, they can create movements that drive change. Building a supportive network of like-minded individuals will amplify their efforts, fostering collaboration that leads to innovative solutions for societal issues. Emphasizing empathy and inclusivity in their leadership style will further enhance their ability to make a lasting impact.

Health and wellness are foundational elements that Life Path 8 individuals must prioritize, as their well-being directly influences their capacity to contribute to society. By maintaining a balanced lifestyle and addressing their physical, mental, and emotional health, they can sustain the energy and resilience needed for their endeavors. Encouraging others to embrace healthy practices not only benefits their personal lives but also cultivates a culture of wellness within their communities. This holistic approach ensures that their contributions are sustainable and impactful.

Finally, building a legacy is an essential consideration for Life Path 8 individuals. Their drive for success often includes a desire to leave a mark on the world. By focusing on creating meaningful contributions, they can construct a legacy rooted in service and positive change. Whether through mentorship, philanthropy, or advocacy, Life Path 8 individuals have the opportunity to influence future generations. By integrating their ambitions with a commitment to societal betterment, they can master their destiny in a way that enriches both their lives and the lives of others.

www.ingramcontent.com/pod-product-compliance
Lightning Source LLC
Chambersburg PA
CBHW060532030426
42337CB00021B/4220